Memories
of Little Cubie

as told by Maranda Katherine Austin Shrum

William Shrum

authorHOUSE®

AuthorHouse™
1663 Liberty Drive
Bloomington, IN 47403
www.authorhouse.com
Phone: 1 (800) 839-8640

Published by AuthorHouse   04/01/2016

ISBN: 978-1-5049-8549-9 (sc)
ISBN: 978-1-5049-8548-2 (e)

Print information available on the last page.

Any people depicted in stock imagery provided by Thinkstock are models, and such images are being used for illustrative purposes only.
Certain stock imagery © *Thinkstock.*

This book is printed on acid-free paper.

This book is the memories of my mother Marandy Katherine Austin Shrum. My name is William (Bill) Shrum, a published author from Stuttgart, Arkansas.

The first photo Hettie White Austin (from left) and her husband Henry Austin taken July 4, 1969 on their 50th Wedding Anniversary

(WRITER AND EDITOR'S NOTE)

Through the years, my brother and I have heard all of the stories, names of the people and the happenings of "Little Cubie." To my mother, who is 85 years of age and will be 86 when this book is published, the memories and images are still real.

This a work of love from my mother who dictated it to me as the best she could remember. It is a gift from her to the future generations who have no idea what the "Greatest Generation" endured.

There are a number of things that a number of my cousins have never heard of and some may think never happened but they did. My mother has told them many times to my brother and me.

"LITTLE CUBIE"

The community was settled around the end of the 19th century, with several families moving to that section of land. It was several miles from DeWitt in the rural area of Arkansas County and was sparsely populated.

"Little Cubie," which is also called "Sunnyside Community" was back then in the woods. There was not much farm land cultivated like there is now, because not too many people back then had modern machinery.

Some people in DeWitt or near DeWitt don't know where it is or how it got it's name. It is right off Highway 1, which leaves DeWitt and goes to Gillett. The road is now called Airport Road, which is paved now, but back when my mother and all of her siblings were growing up, it was called "The Big Road."

"It was nothing but made out of dirt, no gravel and in the Winter time or Spring when it rained, it was nothing but mud." "Now it is gravel up to the where the house was at."

"There were no automobiles back then, in fact mama and daddy never learned how to drive a car."

"My mama could drive a team of horses though, believe me."

(EDITOR'S NOTE) The story of how "Little Cubie" got its' name is when I asked Mr. C.P. Vittitow in 2003 about how "Little Cubie got its' name and he told me this story.

"There was someone who lived down there in that area who fought in the Spanish and American War in the turn of the century. They asked him where he was going back to after the War?"

"He said he was going to Little Cubie."

They lived on a farm, that was 80 acres of land that belonged to Hettie White Austin as a gift from her father. Each sibling was given 40 acres and the extra 40 acres of land she had was from her half sister Nonie Huckaby.

"I have no idea how they got the extra 40 acres."

There are two sets of family members. The White side from Grandfather Robert Lee White with his wife Mrs. Indie White and Grandmother Maggie Hornbeck, later Mrs. Johnny Hornbeck.

The story from my grandmother was she had no full brothers and sisters and was the only child of Maggie Hornbeck and Robert Lee White.

"She was raised in the same household of Robert Lee White and Mrs. Indie White." "She went to DeWitt schools and learned how to cook in the White household."

"Mama told me that the oldest girl of the White family, her sister Doshie was the one that practically raised her." "She said nothing about Mrs. Indie White at all." "She never said that they would say things about her but she did learn how to do things like they were taught in those days as if she did belong in that family."

When she was about 16 years of age, she met a young man from over at Ethel along the river, after the war, who was trapping, logging, learning how to survive and live off the land.

James Henry Austin was his name and a young Hettie White met him, who had just returned from World War I and living near the Ethel community.

He was 26 years of age and she was turning 17 years of age two days later after they were married on July 4, 1919

(Writer's Note) "My grandfather told me before he died around 1969 or 1970 that when he met her, she was the prettiest thing he had ever seen." "I knew I was in love with her when I saw her."

"Isaac William Austin was my Dad's father, who had moved in with them before I was born and who died in 1936, when I was six years old." "I called him Grandpa Will."

"He called me Rand." I think he called his first wife that while they courted and after they were married."

"I was named after her, Maranda Katherine Austin, however on the birth certificate has the name of Marandy Katherine Austin."

"I remember some things they told me, he was a farm hand at the old Winchester farm on Highway 35 between Sheridan and Benton, Ark." "She was a farmers daughter, however because of she being a girl, the girls back then went with the husband and didn't stay too much with the girl's family.

"I remember being the apple of my grandfather's eye." I could do no wrong and when he died, I was six years old and my world ended."

"So I thought, I was very upset, he was my whole life and I loved him with all my heart."

"I think some of it was I was named after his first wife, Maranda Katherine Winchester Austin." "She is buried in Ethel, I couldn't tell you which cemetery." Way back in the 1950s or early 60s, "Alvin, my brother and daddy said they thought they had found her grave near some old trees." "I really don't know if they found the grave or not, I don't even remember the cemetery."

"My grandfather was way into his 80s, when he died." "That was considered old back then because people just didn't live very long back then at all, like they do now." "He is buried in Hearn Cemetery with a headstone."

Robert Lee White ––––

"He was my grandfather." "I never met him, he died before I was born, found out later that he died sometime in the 1920's." "He was killed while he was sitting on top of his white horse in the country."

(EDITOR'S NOTE) We found a photo of him years later with Mrs. Indie Davis White, but no photos of he and Maggie Hornbeck. There is a photo of Robert Lee White, down at Arkansas Post, probably around the 1920s, probably just before his death.

Charley Shrum taken during the war, he finished World War II as a Sergeant.

At a reunion in 1979 at Camp Doughboy.

(Back row, from left) Maranda Austin Shrum, Kirby Austin, Alvin Austin and Jr. Austin.

(Front row, from left) Birtie Austin McDaniel, Katie Austin McGhee, Hettie White Austin, Mattie Wilma Austin and Shirley Austin Murphy.

Taken around 1945 or 1946

Kirby Austin and Katie Austin (Twins)

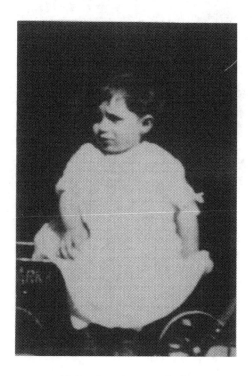

Alvin Austin as a baby

Taken around 1919 or 1920, the time they were married. Hettie White Austin and Henry Austin.

J. R. Austin (left) and his nephew, Kirby DeWayne Austin
(approximately 1951 or 1952)

Marandy Austin (Taken in 1946 in DeWitt
photography studio)

Taken in July of 1956. Taken at the old home place in "Little Cubie."

(Front row, from left) Bill Shrum, Rodger Shrum and Lorraine McGhee Jordan.

(Back row, from left) Etta Darlene Austin Cunningham, Kirby Austin and Henry Austin.

Maggie Hornbeck ———

"She was my grandmother." "I remember seeing her several times, even though, I wasn't supposed to do that, I went ahead and did." "She was a very petite woman, with dark black hair."

"She was in her 50s or 60s when I saw her." "I would slip off and see her and see what she was doing." "I think the reason we weren't supposed to see her was she gave my mama away, but she really didn't, my grandfather just took her to his house." "We were never supposed to see my grandmother, but I would slip off to see her.

(EDITOR'S NOTE) She had a little girl who she was raising in her later years by the name of Peggy DeVore. That was her married name. There is a photo of Maggie Hornbeck in her later years, that I acquired from one of my found relatives that I wouldn't give anything for. She is buried along side of her husband, Johnny Hornbeck in the DeWitt City Cemetery.

Hettie White Austin (1902 - 1990- James Henry Austin (1893- 1975) They were married on July 4, 1919 in "Little Cubie" with a Fourth of July Wedding Celebration.

James Henry Austin was born in 1893 in Ethel, because they had moved from the rural Sheridan area. There were a lot of children, several of the children died in childbirth, which was very common in those days. Maranda Katherine Winchester Austin died around 1898 of childbirth complications. Isaac William Austin remarried a woman, by the name of Jennie, who raise the children, who eventually left the home. Jennie died in the 1920's. Alvin, the oldest of the Austin children does not remember Jennie Austin at all.

The Austin children we know about, who are from Maranda Winchester Austin and Issac William Austin are Hudie, who died in the 1970s, who had no children and had lived briefly with Henry and Hettie because she had no where else to go.

She remained with them on Quartermous Street, until she had to be replaced in a local nursing home in De Witt.

"She always told my daddy that the only thing he could raise was Hell and kids." She said that the day she died.

"He had another sister named Birtie Ozella Austin, who my sister Birtie is named after her."

That is about all I know about that side of the family.

15

(Editor's Note)

The Austin Children:

Marandy was the middle girl in this family, which resided on a farm southeast of DeWitt in the community known for years as "Little Cubie." She had an older brother, Alvin, who locals called him "Babe", Kirby, Katie and Shirley were the older ones also.

"There were two older children, John Henry and Opal, who died from diarrhea and both are buried at Hearn Cemetery." "They were born before Alvin was."

The younger siblings of my mother's are Birtie, Mattie Wilma and J.R.

"Back then, parents had kids to help on the farm," she said. "That was the way it was back then, we were expected to work."

"We were also expected to go to school at least to the 8th grade."

All of the children who grew up to adulthood graduated from Sunnieside School."

"The school was given to the district by my Aunt Fannie," she said. "It was there for the community as long as it was used as a school."

The school was also used as a church and closed down in 1952 or 1953. The structure stood until the 1960s, when the school district wanted the land, not the school on which it was built. "Aunt Fannie wouldn't budge from the agreement." "One night, in the middle of the night, the school house burned." "No one saw nothing." "The church was rebuilt at another location, just down the road from the actual sight."

Issiac William Austin

Issiac William Austin was my Dad's father, who had moved in with them before my mother was born and who died in 1936, when she was six years old.

"He was way into his 80s, when he died."

"He was old back then, people didn't live to be old back then, like they do now."

"My world ended that day." "I was very upset, he was my life and I loved him with all my heart."

"I think some of it was I was named after his first wife, Maranda Katherine Winchester Austin."

WHEN I WAS BORN

"All we need is another mouth to feed," Marandy Austin Shrum always heard in the family.

She knew times were hard on the farm and knew that she was going to have to work during her growing up years.

"Even though the times were hard and tough, everyone else had hard times and maybe even harder."

Her nickname growing up was "Skeeter." This nickname was given by her mother because as she was growing up, she became tall and on the skinny side.

The sister who was born in 1932, was Birdtie Ozella and was called "Pet".

"She was called that for obvious reasons, because she was the pet." "Daddy gave her that nickname."

The families who lived down there in "Little Cubie"

These families lived on the Big Road near the Henry and Hettie Austin's old home place.

•••••••• The Huckaby's lived next house going down the Big Road towards the Austin home on the other side was Uncle Huck and Aunt Fannie. "They had four or five kids, can't remember their names at all. They were all my cousins." "The old house in which they all lived in is still there." "The school house stood not too far from their old homeplace down on the same side."

••••••••••• Dewey Stephens and his wife Aunt Ethel White Stephens had three kids, Naomie, Ruth and Raymond." "These kids were also my cousins."

•••••••••• Next to them lived Mr. and Mrs. Bill Cordell, with kids and next to them were Ray Watkins, his mother and his wife.

•••••••••• Up the hill down the Big Road was Uncle Hollis and Aunt Bessie White. "They had two or three kids, who were already grown but had one boy somewhere around our age, Roscoe."

•••••••• "There was Mrs. Nellis Mae Simpson, a widower, who had I think seven kids three daughters, Mertie, Virginia and Gerstine and four sons, Leon, Travis, Glendon and Wayne. Their house was on down on the other side of the street. "She was no kin to us at all." "Daddy felt sorry for her and would take food to her because she had so many kids and no husband."

•••••••• On down the road, which made a left turn and then a right turn was the Adams House, Mr. and Mrs. Adams. "That is all we called them." "She was the midwife down there."

•••••••• "The Clarks lived down there with along the Adams' "Mr. and Mrs., Clark lived down there and they had nothing but girls, around five of them."

•••••••• Back up the big road coming back down toward the Austin old homeplace was the Dumonds. "There was a boy the same age as my youngest brother, JR." "They were always together.

•••••••• Next was the Ruffin's home. "There was Guy and Hettie Ruffin." "They had two boys, Vern Ruffin and Ralph Ruffin." "Ralph became Alvin, my oldest brothers best friend and he and his wife would visit Ralph and his wife, Hazel quite often in the later years." "They also had four girls, Hestir, Estelle, Loraine and one of the girls was my best friend, Marji Ruffin."

•••••••••• Go on down past the school house and turn right, "Mrs. Alice Simpson, the school teacher at "Little Cubie" had two kids, who all lived there, with no husband for her or father for the kids." "The kids' names were James and Betsie, who also was my best friend."

•••••••••• On the little corner down the Big Road was Mr. and Mrs. Charles Hearn. "They had a son named Buddy."

•••••••••• Next door, but a little ways down the road on the left going back up the Big Road was Jim and Mattie Mae Watkins. "They had a daughter, just a little younger than me, maybe my sister Birtie's age, name Gladys Watkins." "Gladys later married Buddy Hearn and stayed in "Little Cubie." I think Mr. and Mrs. Watkins had another child named Billy Jo."

•••••••••• Right on a little ways was John and Mary Eason. Their kid's names were John Etta, Harvey, Lois, Travis and Lorraine.

•••••••••• Down from them was another Eason home, who had a daughter named Hazel and she married Ralph Ruffin.

"There were alot of kids down there." "We all knew one another, walked with each other to school." "It wasn't very far at all."

AT HOME ••••••••••••••

There was no refrigeration, there were no lights, until the late 1940's, when Rural Electric began doing service down there. There was no indoor plumbing for water and there was no bathroom either. "I was already gone when the modern things came to "Little Cubie." "But it wasn't long after that that they moved from the old homeplace."

Without electricity, there were no electric lights. Coal Oil Lamps lightened everything and there was a battery powered radio that was used very little. "Daddy listened to the radio for news and weather and sometimes if we were all lucky, we would listen to some programs and also "WSM Grand Ole Opry" on Saturday nights."

"Daddy also liked "Just Plain Bill" and Fibber MCGhee and Molly."

"We had to save things from being spoiled, remember no refrigeration." "There was an ice man, who ran up to the "Big Road," about every two or three days." "Ice came in one large block, maybe a nickel, not anything more I think." That was used for our milk, cheese, butter, something like that all placed in a hole in the ground with ice wrapped around the food in cold water."

"We usually had it hid in a shed not far from the house, because critters would come up if it wasn't secure and take our food."

"Meat was always salted and was also kept in a safe place too. So the food would not leave (other people taking it) or disappeared (Sometimes visitors at the house would take them.)"

If things like this did happen, "Daddy would always say that I guessed they were hungry." "These are hard times."

There were two gardens, a medium size garden next to the house, not very far, then there was a "Truck Garden," which was located in the back of the house, a little distance from everyone.

"Believe me, we picked everything from those two gardens." "We placed every kind of vegetable known to man on cycles of the seasons and we collected those for our own use." "We had a variety of fruit trees, apple trees, pear trees and pecan trees." We would pick them when they became ripe in the season of the year."

"We also gathered berries, Blackberries, Dooberries."

We always had some kind of meat, because Kirby would have to kill our meat for that particular meal. "When we were getting low on meat, Mama would say 'Kirby, we need something for supper and he knew exactly what he had to do."

"Mama would also save eggs for Saturday, approximately eight dozen of them, when we went to town to sell to the grocery stores or restaurants for cash money to buy things that we needed for the house." "We had to be careful with the eggs and there were no cartons." "She also sold butter to the town merchants because we made our own."

Kirby was also the trapper of the family. "He would trap anything and everything around there and sell it." "He was supposed to do it in season, but sometimes he would forget." "He would skin the animal, let the hide dry in the back of the house and then take it to town for sale." "That is how we lived, we would use the money for personal expenses for the house." "We also made our own butter from a mold." "We had about 10 pounds which Mama would sell to restaurants, even other people in town and grocery stores."

Every year we would buy little chicks, usually in the Spring of the year from Bogards in Stuttgart." "We didn't come to Stuttgart, they usually sent the chicks to another store in DeWitt and we would pick them up always on a Saturday."

"The food would may not be what we liked, but we had plenty of food back then." "Some people down there didn't have so much."

"There were three meals served and we had all three of them. We had BREAKFAST, we had DINNER and we had SUPPER." "If some of the older kids had something special to do, Mama would save something for them, but if they just missed it by goofing around, no supper." "She didn't go for that, you were there when it was served. We didn't miss many meals."

"Milk was from a cow, not from a carton, we didn't know what a carton of milk was until I moved to town to work at the Rowland's." "We had around 10 milk cows and my Mama always milked the cows." "She knew how to do it, it wasn't an easy job." "We also sold milk, which my Daddy placed in gallon cans along he road and the people would pick them up on the side of the Big Road." "This happened every other day."

CANNING:

This is a way of preserving things that the younger generation has no clue. "By the time I came along, Mama was already canning." "She would buy about one dozen of glass jars each year at Ferguson's, I think they were on the Square back then." "Everything went in them, vegetables, fruits, just no meat."

"Everyone helped with the Canning." "That was a big job." "Every glass jar had to be boiled clean, then dried, placed the contents in the jar and seal the jar." "Most of the time the top sealed and sometimes it didn't and the contents would spoil. You would just loose that product."

"Fruit tasted so good in a pie at Christmas or when snow was on the ground." "That was a special treat."

DAYS of the WEEK ACTIVITIES

Monday — "This was wash day, all day long." (Remember no washing machines here or dryers)

Tuesday — "Iron Day"

Wednesday — More Ironing"

Thursday — "Finishing the Ironing" (The reason this took so long, remember no electricity, this required hot irons on the stove. The use of three or four continuously).

Friday — "This was Clean House Day."

Saturday — "Play Day and Bath Day" —— —— —— "Everyone took a bath to greet the church, the next day and the week"). "Water had to be pumped from the well to a bucket to place in the tub." "I was the one responsible for all of the pumping of the water." "If it wasn't done, they would call "Marandy, you slacking on your job." "I don't know who had volunteered me to do that in the first place, but I wished they had never done it." "I must had done it at an early age, because I never can remember when I didn't until I left home, then Mattie Wilma said she was volunteered that job."

Sunday — "Church" "This was sometime around 9:30 a.m. for Sunday School and then Church". "Reverend Luther Davis was the pastor."

(EDITOR'S NOTE) "Rev. Davis is the one who married, my Dad, Charley Shrum and my mother Maranda Katherine Austin Shrum on Oct. 30, 1949.

"We usually got out around 12:30 or if we had a visiting preacher, we might get out at 1 p.m., just nothing later." "Then it was time for Dinner, Sunday Dinner."

GOING TO TOWN

"This was an all day affair." "It involved horses, a wagon and a select of kids who went with Daddy and Mama." "Not all of the kids went at the same time, we alternated." "About two kids at a time on Saturdays." "I always went to the library, which was in the basement of the Courthouse." "I would check out books, mostly Nancy Drew Mysteries, I loved to read them." I read everyone of them, there was a series of them." "I think I liked them because she was a teenager, just like me solving mysteries."

"If it wasn't my time to go to town, Mama would take my books back and sometimes check me out another book." "I was always reading."

This was the time she would go to town to sell her eggs, butter and whatever she had extra to sell." "Daddy would park the horses and wagon just off the Square and sometimes, he would be told to move them, but he always told the police that he would when he was through with getting his supplies."

"They didn't do it every Saturday, just some Saturday's. He wouldn't pay any attention to them anyway." "Also back then, Daddy would slip off and go to one of those beer joints and drink a little and even get a bottle." Mama didn't know exactly if he was doing that and that night, he would be pretty bad by then and there would be a fight." "It didn't happen too often, but it did happen."

"The stores would be open until 12 midnight back then." "That was just the way it was, so everyone could come to town and shop at the stores."

(EDITOR'S NOTE) When I grew older in the 1950s and went down to DeWitt on a number of occasions with our parents, I do remember on several occasions that the Square was very busy. They may have not been open say 12 midnight when I came along in the mid or late 1950s, but on Saturday nights, the shops were open around 9 or at least until 10 p.m.

WORKING ON THE FARM

Back in the day, owners of the farms around here had children, who were to grow up and work on the farm at all kinds of capacity. "We worked back then." "There were specific jobs for us to do." "Some of the girls worked on the farm doing a number of duties, such as helping Mama with the garden, collecting fruit from the trees, canning, cooking, cleaning, things like that." "We all worked, we had too."

"Daddy worked in the fields and when the boys got older, they helped him with the crops. "Sometimes Mama had to help Daddy in the fields, especially when the boys were growing up and not quite old enough to help." "When they got old enough, then the boys were in the field."

The horses we had were Topsy and Dollie. "Topsy was the work horse and Dollie was the recreational horse or the wagon horse with Dollie."

"I did all of the above except, cooking, that was Mama's job and she had some help from Aunt Nonie." "When my sister Katie got bigger, she was taught how to cook by the women and boy, could she cook."

(EDITOR'S NOTE) "She always made chocolate cakes for us, when she baked for other people at pot lucks or at special occasions, such as birthday parties, from scratch and with homemade icing."

"That is when I started dating Charley Shrum, the first thing I told him was I didn't know how to cook." "He just smiled and said, I will show you."

(EDITOR'S NOTE) He learned how to cook in the Army, when he was in World War II, especially when he returned in 1947, when he had enlisted in the service after the War."

"As I have mentioned earlier, my job was primarily pumping water, but I did tend to the cotton as I grew older." "I was the best cotton picker around all of "Little Cubie." "That is what the other people and older adults always said." "They said my rows were always left clean and I had more weight in the bags than any of the other kids around there."

"At one time, the other people around there thought I could beat this one woman from around Phillips County, up north of us." "I was still a little girl and she was a woman and the place was at Elaine." "Daddy wouldn't let me go up there, because he still remembered the trouble they had around Elaine and Helena in 1919 and he really didn't want me up there." "So I never found out if I was that good."

CHRISTMAS AT LITTLE CUBIE

"We always went out and cut down our Christmas Tree, around one week before Christmas." "We all decorated it with paper streamers, cut out of a catalog or newspaper and popcorn strung around the tree." "We never put any candles on the tree, they were too dangerous, they may catch the tree on fire."

"We saw Santa Claus on the Square in DeWitt every year." "We told him what we wanted him to bring us."

"We always got one toy each year of Christmas," "We always got the present on the morning of Christmas." "The girls got dolls and the boys got trucks or a 'BB Gun." "We also got some hard Christmas candy, that came in a five-gallon bucket." "We also got fruit, oranges, apples and all kinds of nuts." "That was the only time we got things like that, at Christmas time."

"Daddy loved Christmas, he made sure we had Christmas." "He always said Christmas was for kids."

SCHOOL WITH MISS ALICE

"The school teacher's name was Alice Simpson and a widower, with two children, James and Betsie Simpson."

"During the year, we had all kinds of plays there at the school." "Our mother would always come, but Daddy wouldn't come, because he was working." "Daddy was on the school board while all of us kids were in school."

"We also had Halloween Parties there and we all would dress up in costume." "I would always come as "Being Tacky," which meant I would wear old clothes, such as pants, tack socks on the pants everywhere on me." "We never bought a Halloween costume, didn't know what they were." "That was one thing Daddy would come with Mama, was to the Halloween Parties and I usually won."

"At these special things at school, there was always food." We loved it and everyone in that small community from miles around came." "We also had the year-end of school, same thing, lots of food and plenty of games." "This was at the end of the school year, it was always held outside."

"At Christmas, we had programs." We were always having plays and everyone enjoyed them, this was way before Television." "Sometimes I had a part in the play."

"The school had long windows and doubled as a church on Sundays.

"Also there at school, one year and the only year, I was about 10, I decided to take care of a calf." "I think everyone helped me do this, but I did win a first place blue ribbon at the Arkansas County Fair."

(EDITOR'S NOTE) In 2010, she received an Alumni Award from the Arkansas County 4-H program at the Annual Arkansas County 4-H Banquet for her being in the Sunnyside 4-H Club and was one of the first girls to show a calf at the county fair. At that time, the fair had only been three years old.

When we finished the eighth grade, which was as far as we could go without going to DeWitt to high school." "At the "Little Cubie" school we had graduation at the end of eighth grade and got our certificate, if we wanted to finish high school."

"If you decided to go on to high school in DeWitt, you had be boarded at a home and work to pay off your tuition and books." "I just didn't think I was that smart to do something like that."

"Mrs. Alice taught all grades first grade to eighth grade." Sometimes she would teach a couple of grades together and when this happened, the others would be studying or working on other things."

"We had reading, writing, history, arithmetic, spelling and geography." "I liked all of the subjects except geography, because I told Mrs. Alice, that there were chances I would never go to those other places on the map." "She would say that I may go to those places and besides I needed to know them."

1941???? (Around that time)

(Back row, from left)) Virginia Fuller, unidentified boy and Raymond Stephens.

(Middle row, from left) Mattie Wilma Austin, Virginia Simpson, Marandy Austin, Betsie Simpson and Marjorie Ruffin.

(Front row, from left) Ralph Eason and Billy Bob Gray.

Class of 1918

KubiA School
SANNY SidE School

This is what the school house look like around 20 years earlier.

This photo taken in 1918

The Conflicting Stories of the Gum. ——— "There was one time, when my best friends, Betsie and Mar; put gum in my eye." "It was my eye and the teacher Mrs. Alice had to get it out by using alcohol. "It nearly blinded me." "We still don't know why and we continued to be best of friends, despite that."

(EDITOR'S NOTE) Marji Ruffin Hackney remembered it quite different. "We put gum in her hair and to this day I don't know why, but it sure caused a mess." After telling my mother that story that Marji told, my mother said. "I ought to know what happened, it was my eye."

"The school was a one-room school house, with wooden floors and long windows on both sides." "There was a front door and a back door, with a boot and coat room just to the right of the front door." "The boot and coat room was for the muddy boots and the coats for Winter." "We had to wear boots because it got real muddy."

"We only had a half mile walk to school each day, each way."

"There was a pot-belly stove in the middle of the room and we had an organ." "There was a big blackboard that reached the width of the room which was behind the teacher's desk.":

"We had two rows of desks, the kind that sat two people each." "Our school didn't have a bell tower, so the teacher would use a hand bell to call us in." "There was a water pump in the front yard and a big back yard for recess." "In the back yard, set back a little were the two out houses, one for the girls and one for the boys."

"Some of the games we played were Annie-over, kick the can, jump rope, hop scotch, drop the handkerchief and marbles."

"Marbles was just for boys, they wouldn't let the girls play."

We also had Jumper-Down, this was when someone would get on their all fours and you had to jump over them without touching them or you were it."

"We played baseball and we ran track." "Track was my thing and we ran barefooted." "My feet were tough as nails and I ran fast." "I could even outrun the boys as well as the girls."

"We had races at Point DeLuce during school and I always won ribbons." 'During the summers, hard tracks were fixed at Dough Boy for us to race on." "I wore Number 5 and ran the 50-yard dash and when one time this boy and I kept finishing in a dead heat and they finally gave us both first place blue ribbons."

"My favorite subject was reading, because I loved to read." "It was really the only recreation I had besides playing outside, which was done a lot in the Spring and Summer months."

(EDITOR'S NOTE) Camp Doughboy was a gathering place, which was established by the American Legion after World War I. It is located approximately six miles south of DeWitt on Highway 1 which goes to Gillett. The camp still exists and the main building is named after H. C. Ruffin.

THE MIDWIFE – Mrs. ADAMS

"Mrs. Adams, that is what we called her was the lady who delivered all of the Austin children." "Alvin, my oldest brother always thought that Mrs. Adams had a baby in her little black bag, every time, she came and spent a little time with Mama, a baby appeared." "The bag was just like a doctor's bag and looked like one." "It was black and had all of the things she needed to deliver babies." "She delivered all of the children, from Alvin, the oldest to J.R., the youngest." "Some of the women would always help with the delivery with Mrs. Adams." "The men were never around."

THE WAR YEARS

Prior to World War II, probably in 1939 or 1940, "Alvin Austin, my brother volunteered to be in CC Camp, which was at St. Charles." **(EDITOR'S NOTE)** The Civilian Conservation Corps, which was a federal public work relief program for unemployed, unmarried men from relief families as part of the New Deal. These men ere from the ages of 17 to 28. By 1942, with World War II and the draft in operation, need for work relief declined and Congress voted to close the program. "I remember the money that they earned went to the family." "We sure needed the money back then."

"I remember when they came back, we girls would wear their pants around the farm." "We had to wear them under our dresses but we wore them."

"Kirby was in the United States Navy, he told us he wanted to see the world." "After the war, we wore his bell bottoms also around the farm."

"Katie wanted to enlist in the Wacs, which was a women's version of the Army." **(EDITOR'S NOTE)** Women's Army Corps (WAC) was the women's branch of the United States Army. It was created as an auxiliary unit. It was started in July of 1943 and disbanded in 1978 and all units were integrated with male units.

"Mama and Daddy wouldn't sign the papers and she wasn't allowed to go into the WAC." "I remember how disappointed she was."

"G.W. got killed in world War II, not long after he was shipped over to the War." "A telegram came to us on the farm, in 1942, I think, may have been in the first part of 1943."

"We got all of the news from the War on that battery operated radio and sometimes from leftover newspapers that we got or borrowed from other people."

"We had to ration some things, like sugar, flour and coffee." "We were give ration stamps during the War years."

"We were not unlike any other family in Little Cubie." "We all had to go to war." "The civil service notice that the boys had to go to was at the post office on Cross Street." "The Civil Service officer was a Charles Watkins, I think that was his first name." "He was at that job for at least 30 years, maybe more."

Life After Little Cubie

"I left home to see what the world had to offer." "I didn't go far, just to DeWitt and worked for the Carr family, for just a few months, then I was recommended for a job at the Rowland House-hold." "I was 14 years old."

"The family was George and Mildred Rowland, with his mother and their three children, George Edward, Bill and Glora Belle." "I lived with them, ate with them, went to church with them and did just about everything with them." The ages of the kids when I first started were about 8 for George Edward, 6 for Bill and 2 for Glora Belle. I was only just a few years older than George Edward. "My salary was $1 a day, expenses were paid, except my own clothes, which I had to buy myself."

"The $1 a day was regardless if I worked at the cafe or not."

(EDITOR'S NOTE) The cafe was located in the red brick building on East Cross St., just off the square on the northeast corner, down a little on East Cross St. It is still standing, nothing in it. My mother hasn't heard from the children, any of them since she left them in the fall of 1949, when she married my Dad, Charley Shrum.

"I worked for the Rowland's from 1944 until 1949, when I was married." "The kids didn't like Charley, they always said he was going to take me away."

"During this time, while I worked, I got to know some other girls." "They were around my age, they were Carolyn Calvert, Mary Jean Schallhon and another girl, which I never got her name."

"Mary Jean lived in the old Haliburton House, which was the oldest house in DeWitt." "The other girl Carolyn Calvert, was the daughter of the Calvert's who own a dress shop/mens shop on the Square." "The other girl, who I never knew her name lived right next door or a house down from Mary Jean."

(EDITOR'S NOTE) The other girl, who mother couldn't name was Johnnie Martin, who later married Buddy Leibrock, who had a store on the Square also. Johnnie Martin later became a teacher at DeWitt High School.

"Mr. George wanted me to go back to high school, but I was working for him and really didn't think I could go back after all of those years." "Back then, you still had to buy your own books and there was study time, with three kids." "I just didn't think I could do it."

"I went with a few young men through the years while I was at the Rowland's." "My family wanted me to marry someone down there or in DeWitt and I always told my family that I wasn't going to marry a drunk or one of my cousins." "I was better than that and if it took me longer to find a nice man, then that is what would be."

"I shopped on the Square, back then, it was a busy place." "I would get to see my family when they came to town." "I missed them, but I was OK." "My sisters kept asking me if I was ever going to get married and I told them one of these days." "They laughed at me and told me that no man was going to put up with me and my high flying ways." "I had no idea what that meant."

"I just had some standards and a man to put up with me or I was going on down the road without him."

"I went to church with the Rowland's back then." "I took the kids to Sunday School and George and Mildred would join us later." The church was First Baptist Church, then "We always walked." "I walked everywhere."

(EDITOR'S NOTE) First Baptist Church, the site where my mother went to church was torn down and the current church was built on the same site, around 1980 or in the 1980s.

"I bought my clothes at "Calvert's." "They had the best dresses, they were new and somewhat expensive, but that is what I was working for, so I bought them there." "They were the ones who had the daughter that I knew." "Their daughter, Carolyn wasn't my favorite, the other two girls were much nicer."

(EDITOR'S NOTE) When we were growing up and heard these names, we had no idea who these girls were but as we became older, we found out who they were.

Around the time of 1947 or 1948 Mama became friends with her brother Kirby's first wife Edith Watkins Austin.

"We were very close at one time." "She and I would walk from town back to the home place many times."

Meeting Charley Shrum

"I met Charley Shrum one night on the Square." "It had to be right after Christmas of 1948 and New Years of a 1949." "I didn't know him and he didn't know me."

"Both of us had seen each other on the Square and I knew he wasn't from DeWitt." "I didn't know where he was from, but he wasn't from DeWitt." "I found out that we knew each other's friends, but not one another at all." "We met on the north side of the entrance to the Square."

(EDITOR'S NOTE) This the side of the DeWitt, which is now, th DeWitt Fire Department, the old legion building and the Senior Center. My Dad had always said that my mother was the prettiest thing he had ever seen. "Charley Shrum was the prettiest man I had ever seen."

"When we first started going together, it was sometime around the last of January of 1949, because I always got some boxes of chocolates for Valentines Day." "There were also times we had to bring Margret along, who was Charley's baby sister." "She was three years old."

"The Rowland children liked Charley, but they were so afraid that he would take me away from them." "Mildred, George and Mrs. Rowland (George's mother) really liked Charley and they thought he would make a good husband to me."

"We went together for the rest of the year and was married on Oct. 30, 1949." "We were married at the old homeplace in "Little Cubie." "I told my mama and sisters that I was going to marry him and have a bunch of babies."

"I was not the oldest girl in the Austin family to get married but I was the last one to get married." "I was 19 years old." "I was the only one to get married at the old homeplace."

OTHER THINGS ABOUT CUBIE

The only children to graduate from high school were Katie and JR. Katie went to live with Bo and Nora Dixon and worked for them as she attended DeWitt High School. She graduated in 1945. JR Austin graduated from DeWitt High School in 1956. as they had moved to town by that time and lived at the saw mill northwest of the Square.

Marandy Katherine Austin, who by this time had dropped the y at the end of her first name and added an a, was the only child of eight, who was married at the old home place. The wedding took place on a Saturday, Oct. 30, 1949. "It was raining that day, all day and it was pouring."

"People came from all over the community to come to my wedding, they didn't ever think I was going to get married." "I had already told them I wasn't getting married to a cousin or a drunk."

"I remember saying everyone was there, even Minnie Watkins and she never went anywhere." "At the wedding on the Shrum side was Mr. and Mrs. Shrum and four year old Margret."

"I didn't have a white dress to wear, because I couldn't find one, so I settled on a pale blue dress." "I could have worn a white dress, because of purity being the color."

"We didn't have photographs back then because no one had camera's back then."

"As far as I can remember, I remember hearing about another family living with us, Aunt Nonie and her two sons G.W. (Guy) Huckaby and Marion Huckaby, also a brother of Mama's, Virgil, who was blind."

(Back row, from left) Betty Jane Wheeler and Don Gray.

(Second row from the back, from left) Gladys Watkins, Betty Watkins, Bertie Austin, Dorothy Vaught, Fannie Eason, Travis Simpson and Dorrell Cordell.

(Second row from the front, from left) Unidentified, Wayne Simpson and Walter Harold Durnoud.

(Front row, from left) Mattie Wilma Austin, Donnie Watkins, Unidentified, Elois Vaught and Lois Eason.

(Back row, from left) Howard Gray, Raymond Stevens, Shirley Austin, Myrtie Simpson, Ruby Eason, Loraine Ruffin, Willie Lee Cordell, Virginia Fuller and Virginia Simpson.

(Front row, from left) Unidentified, Billy Bob Gray, Ralph Eason, Betsy Simpson, Marandy Austin and Marjorie Ruffin

(Top row, from left) Evelyn Rodgers, Elsie White, Alvin Austin, Leon Simpson and Stanley Simspon.

(Third Row, from left) Hazel Eason, Vern Ruffin, Kirby Austin and Fay Adams.

(Second row, from left) Dorothy Eason, Ruth Stevens and Hettie Vaughn.

(Front row, from left) Wesley Adams and Beaula Vaughn.

(Back row, from left) Travis Simpson, Raymond Stevens, Virginia Simpson, Marvin Simpson, Glendon Simpson and Leon Simpson.

(Front row, from left) Betsie Simpson, Unidentified ___ __ __ ___ ___, Derstine Simpsson and Wayne Simpson.

(Back row, from left) Fay Adams, Thelma Eason, Hester ruffen, Hazel Eason and Evelyn Rodgers.

(Front row, from left) Katie Austin, Heather Vaughn, Loraine Ruffen and Ruth Stevens.

The lineage of Hettie White Austin

The sisters on the Maggie Hornbeck side:

- Anna Mae (Louis Capps)

- Johnnie (Hynum)

- Linena (Robert Bullock)

Brothers and sisters on the Robert Lee White and Mrs. Inda Davis White

- Doshie (Charlie Vaughn)

- Fannie (Huck Huckaby)

- Nonie (Guy Huckaby)

- Ethel (Dewey Stephens)

- Wesley (Dash) White

- Verge (he was single and a bachelor) White

- Hollis (Bessie) White

Hettie White Austin had no full brothers and sisters, only half brothers or sisters

The lineage of the Austin Children:

Cecil Alvin Austin (July 19, 1923 – Sept. 20, 2014)

Kirby Paul Austin (Oct. 22, 1925 – July 23, 1988)

Katie Pauline Austin McGhee (Oct. 22, 1925 – Jan. 24, 1998)

Shirley Mae Austin Murphy (June 1, 1928 – Jan. 3, 2015)

Marandy Katherine Austin Shrum (July 22, 1930 –)

Birtie Ozella Austin McDaniel (Nov. 19, 1932 –)

Mattie Wilma Austin Young (Feb. 4, 1935 –)

James Henry Austin Jr. (JR) (May 1, 1938 –)

Printed in the United States
By Bookmasters